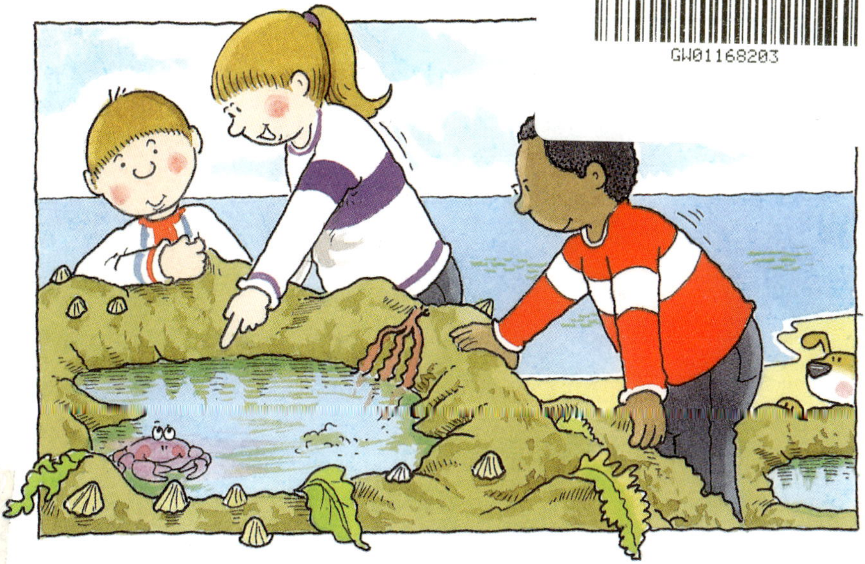

Ben and Pen Rob

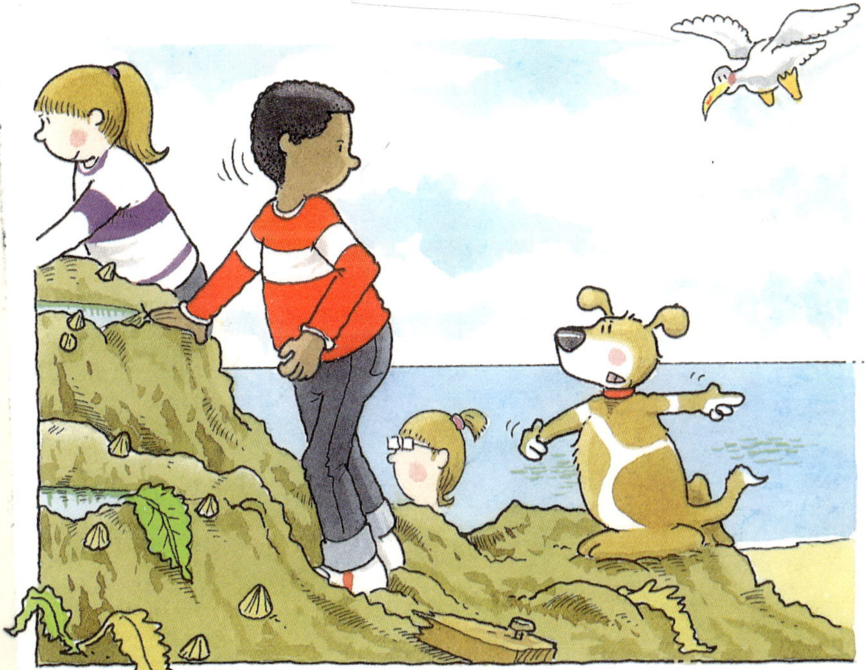

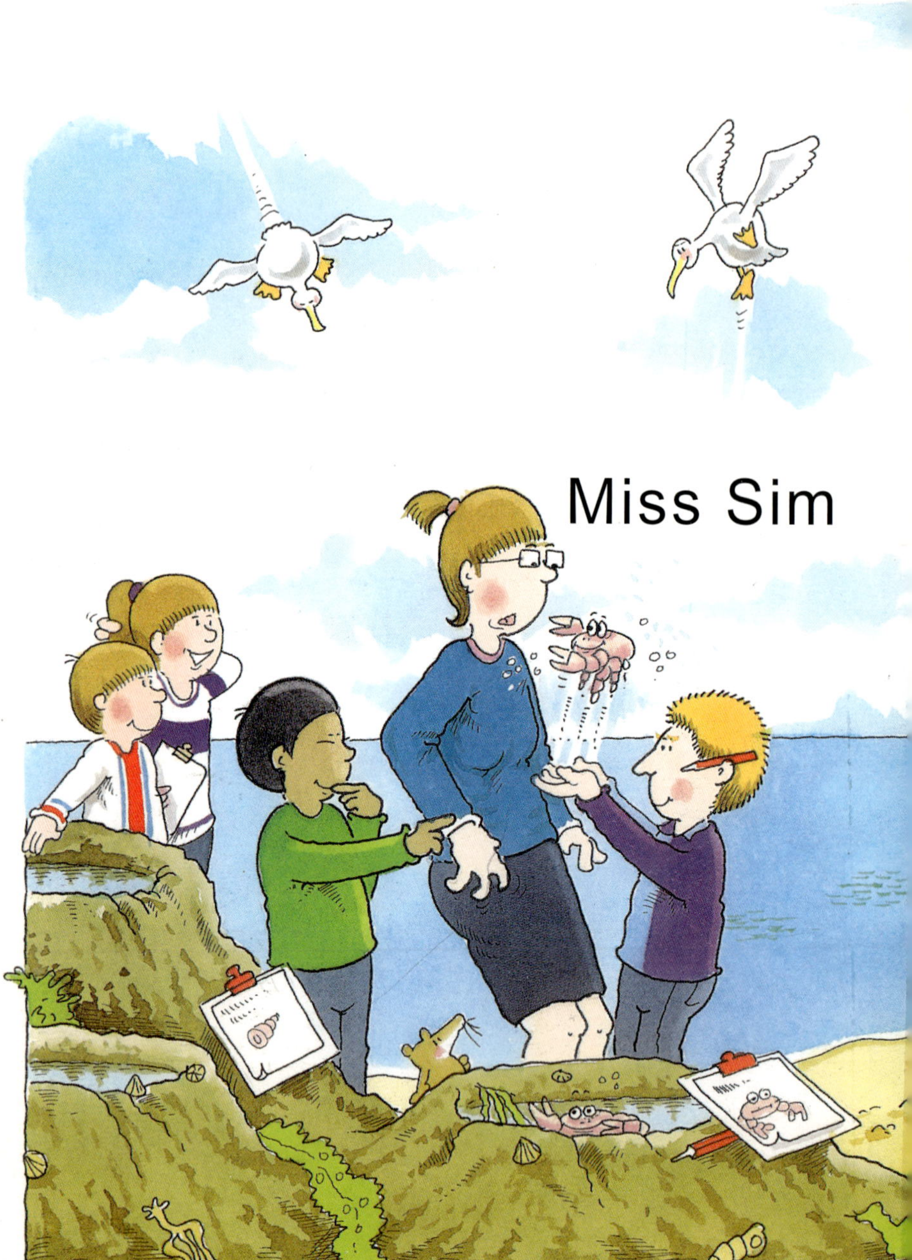

Miss Sim

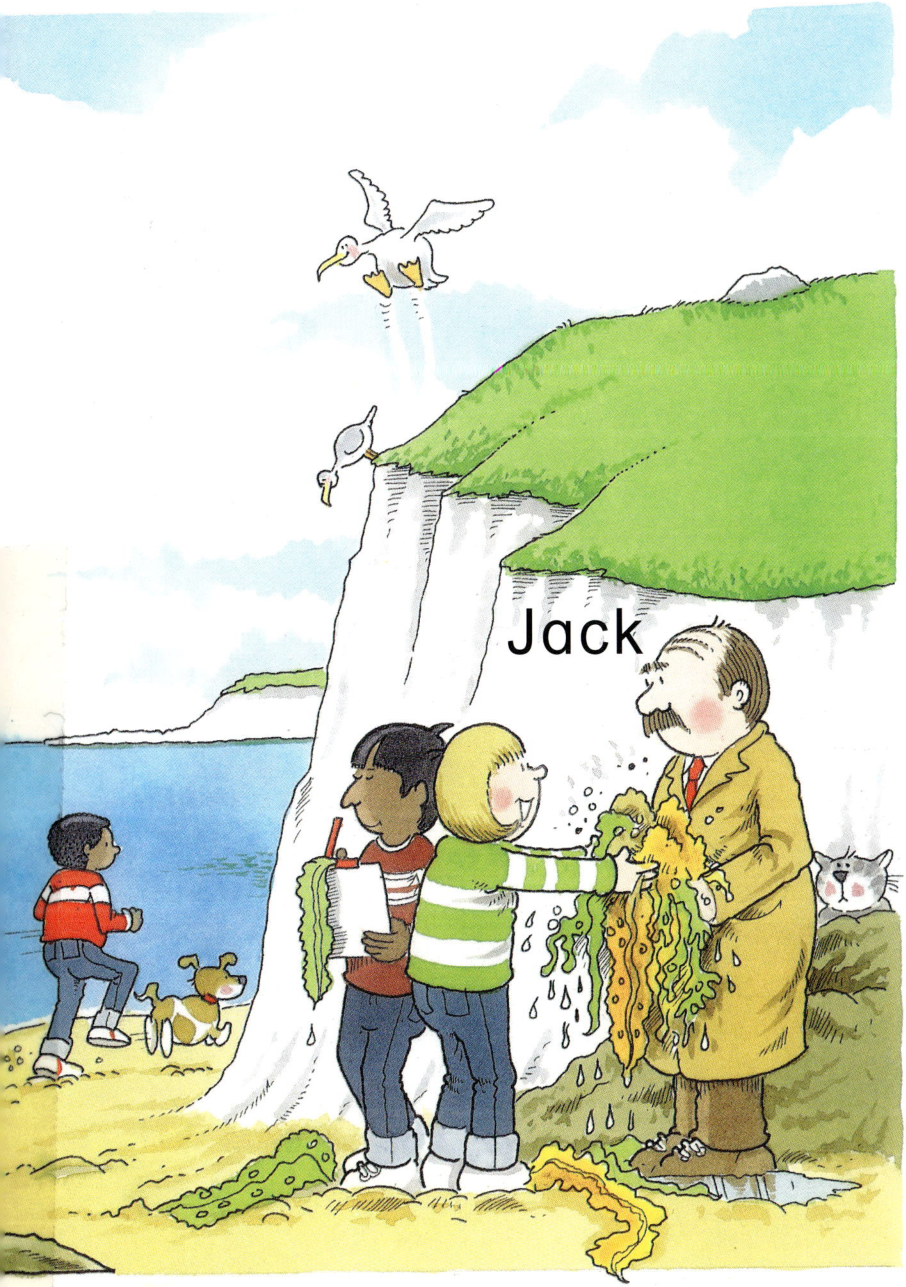

Jack

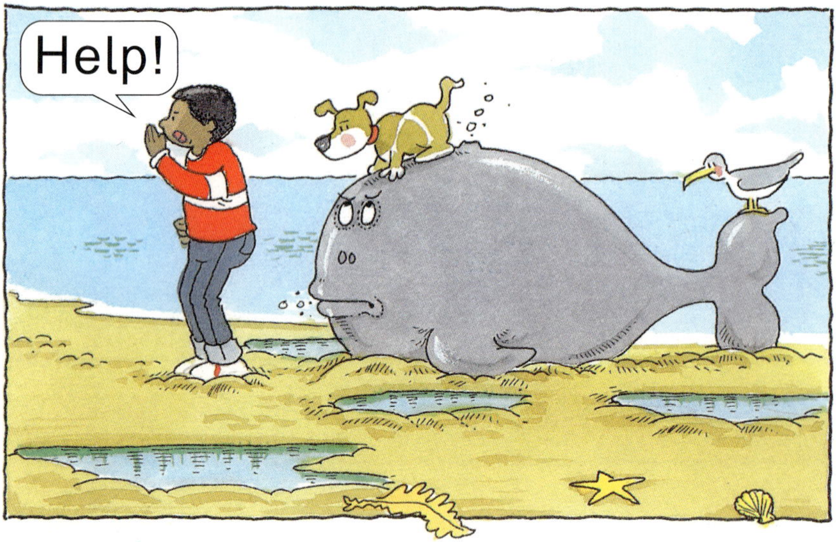

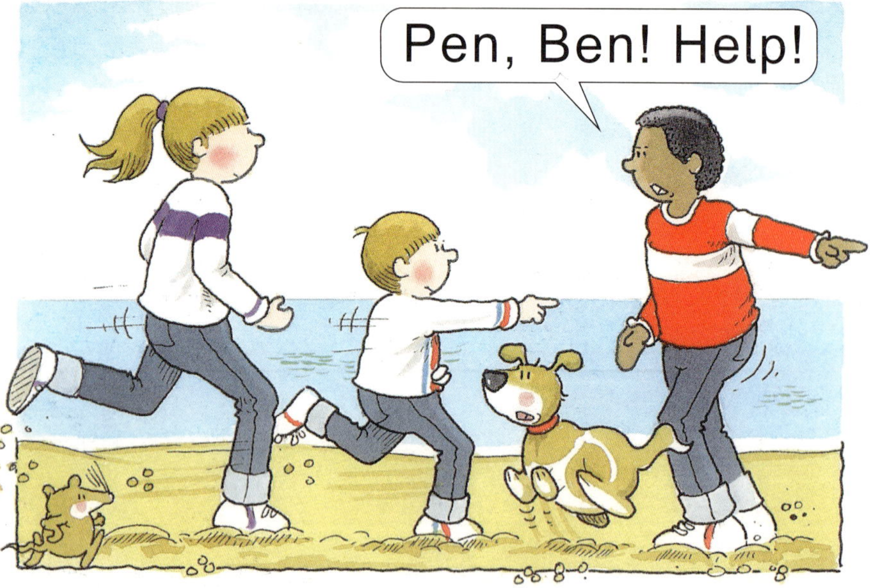

Pen and Ben went to help.

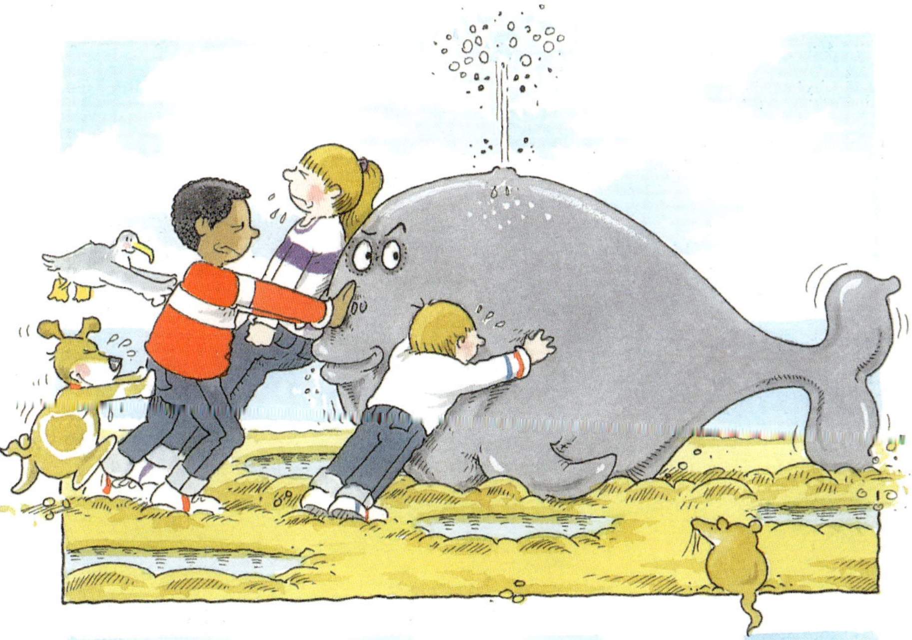

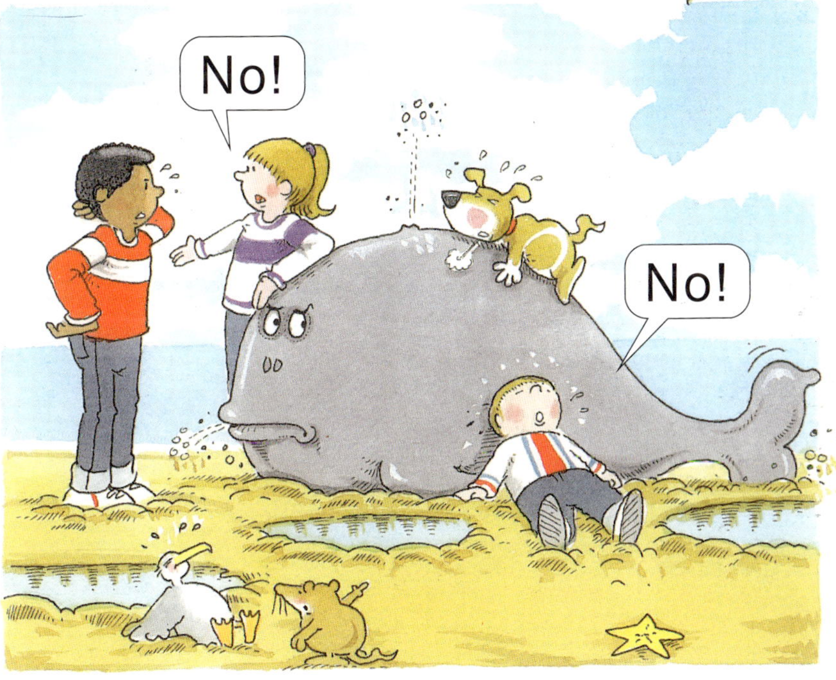
No!
No!

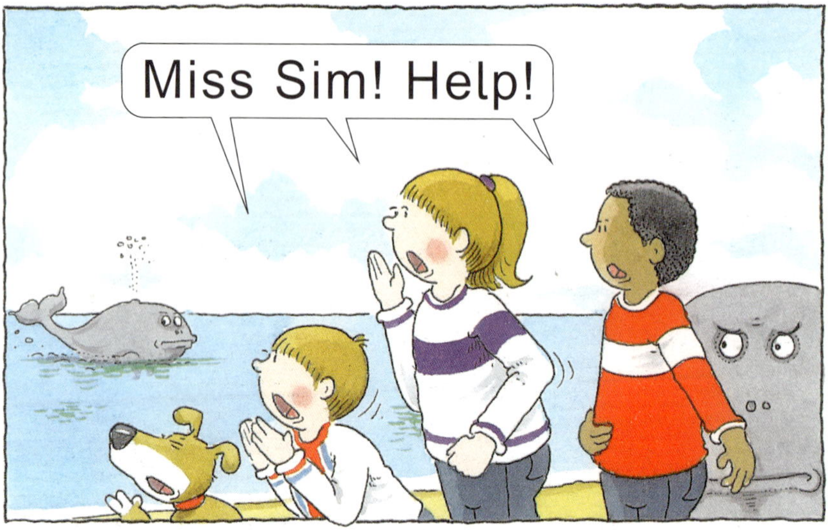

Miss Sim went to help.

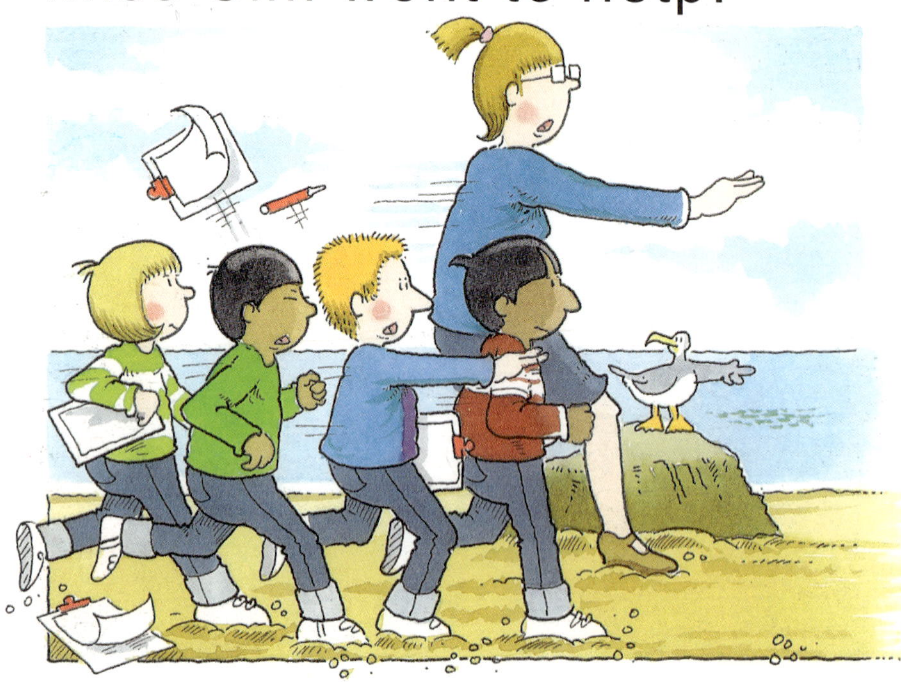

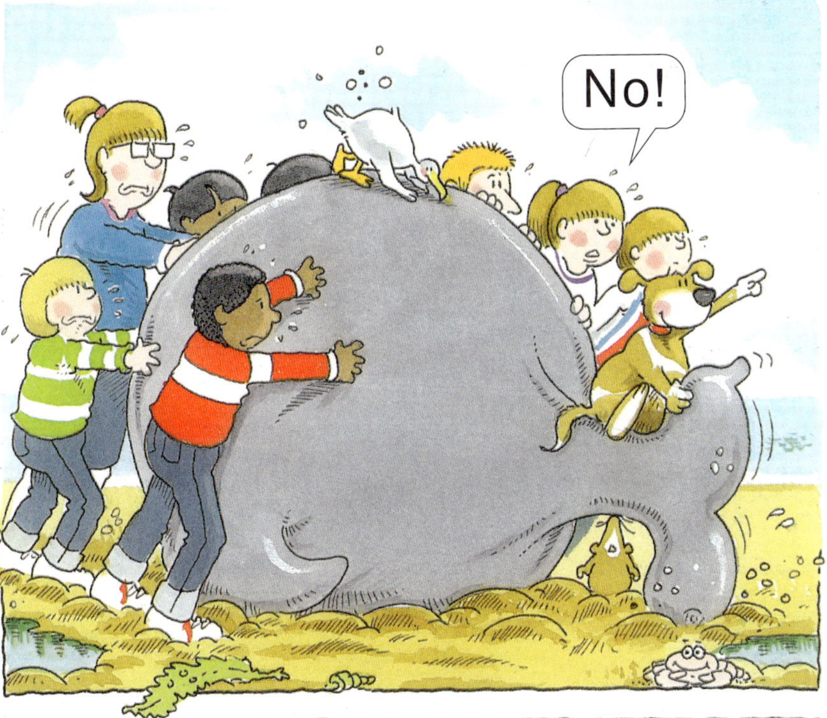
No!

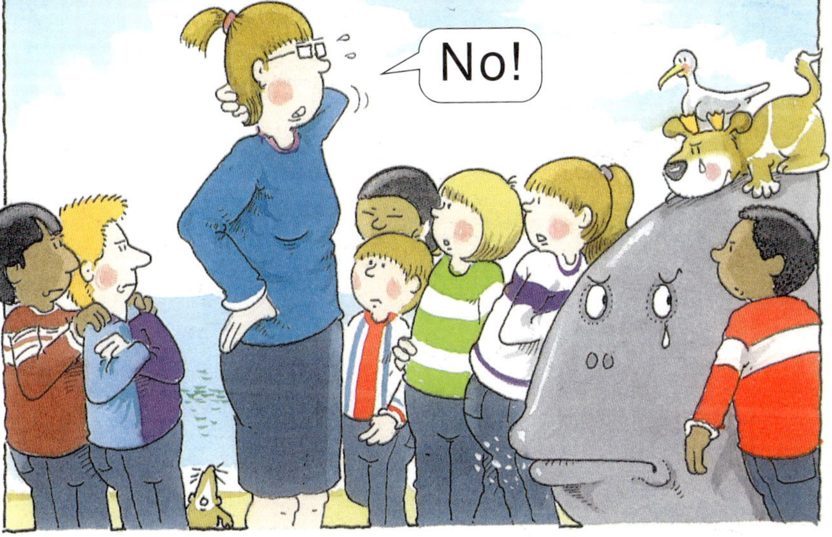
No!

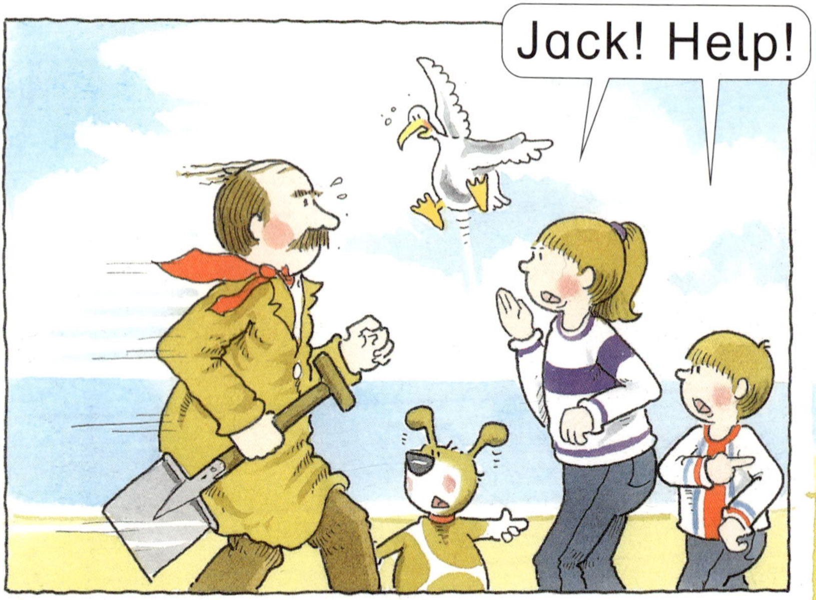
Jack! Help!

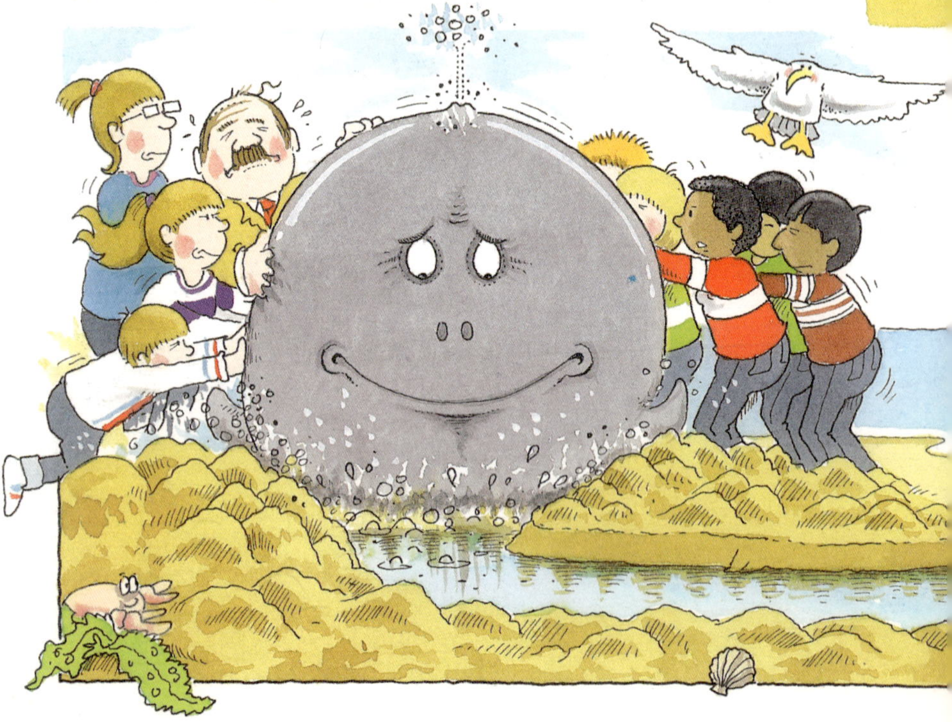

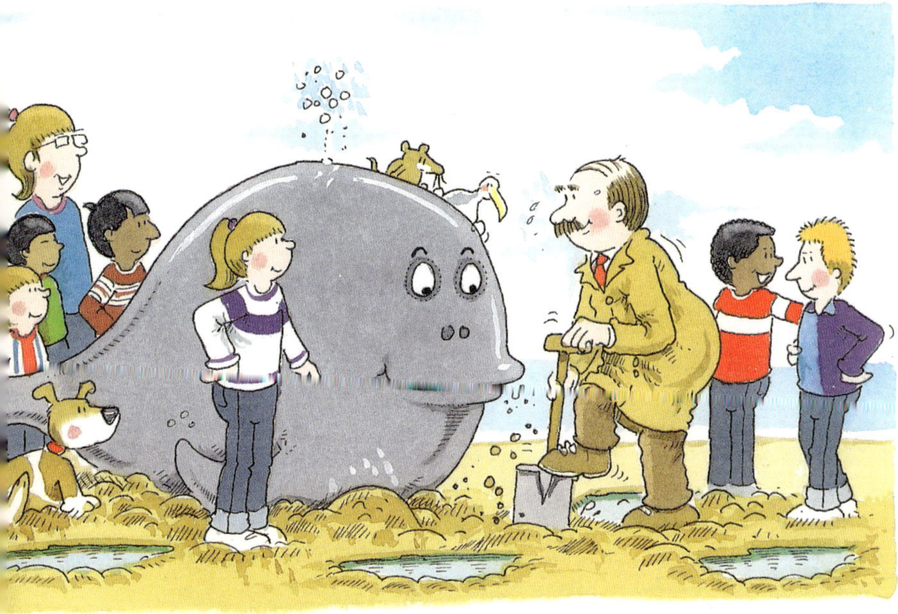

Jack went to help.

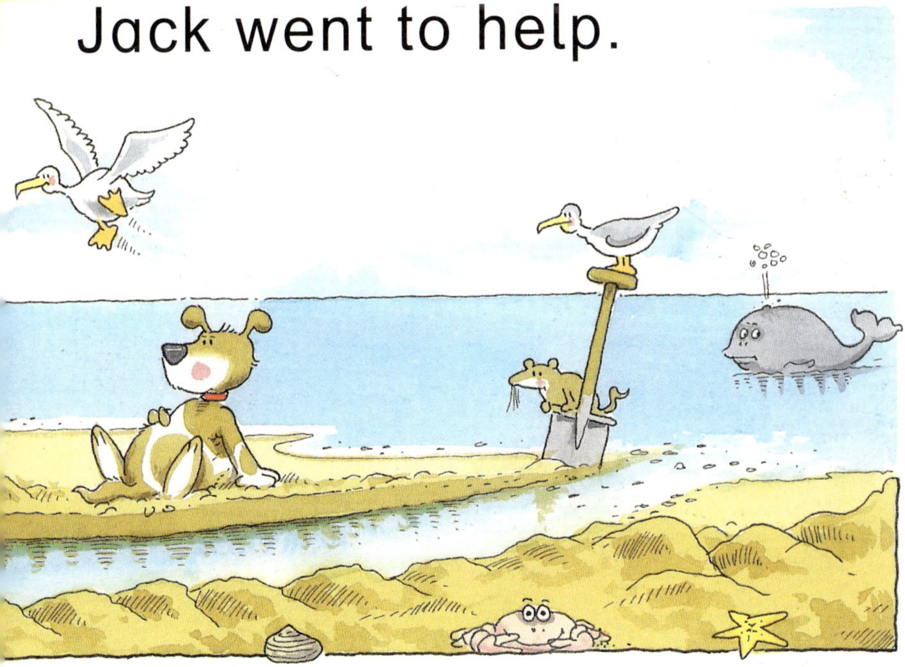

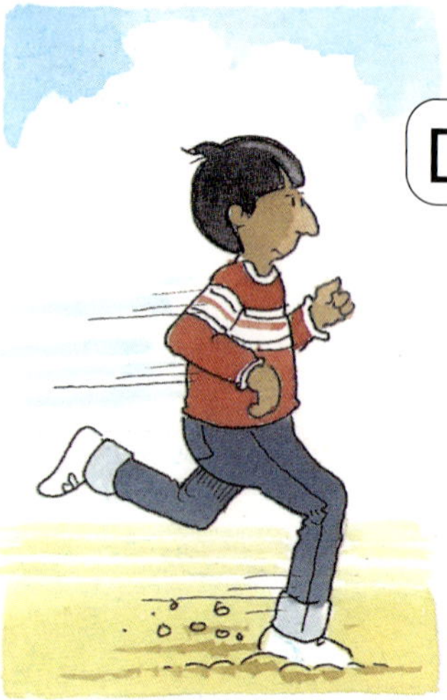

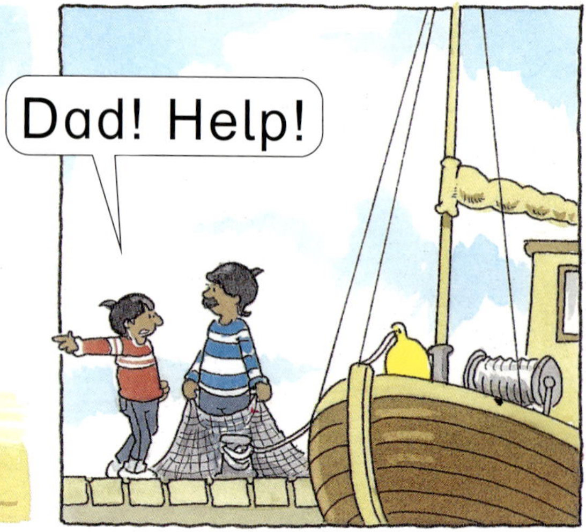

Dad went to help.

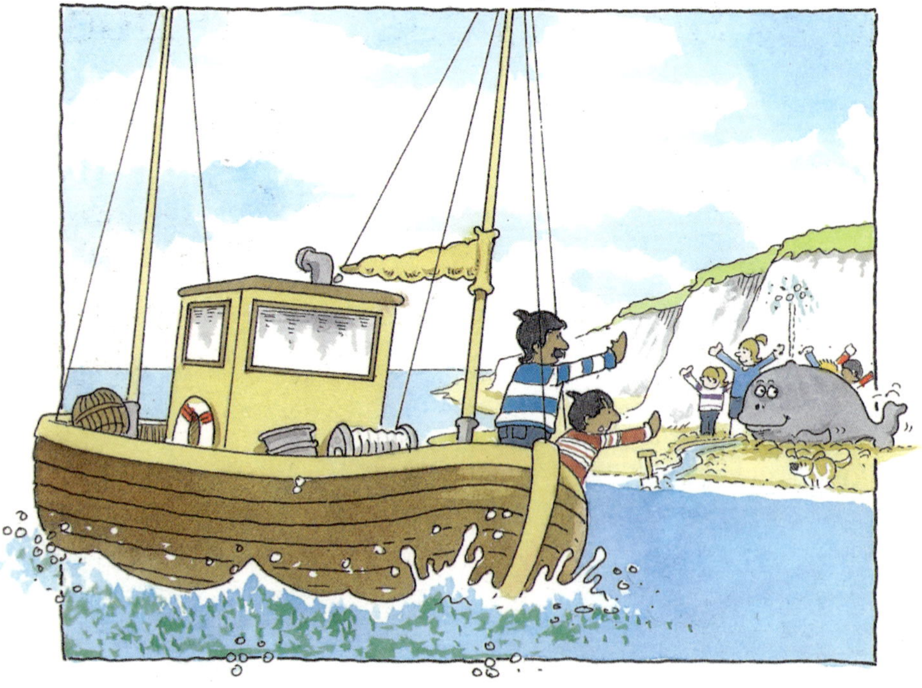

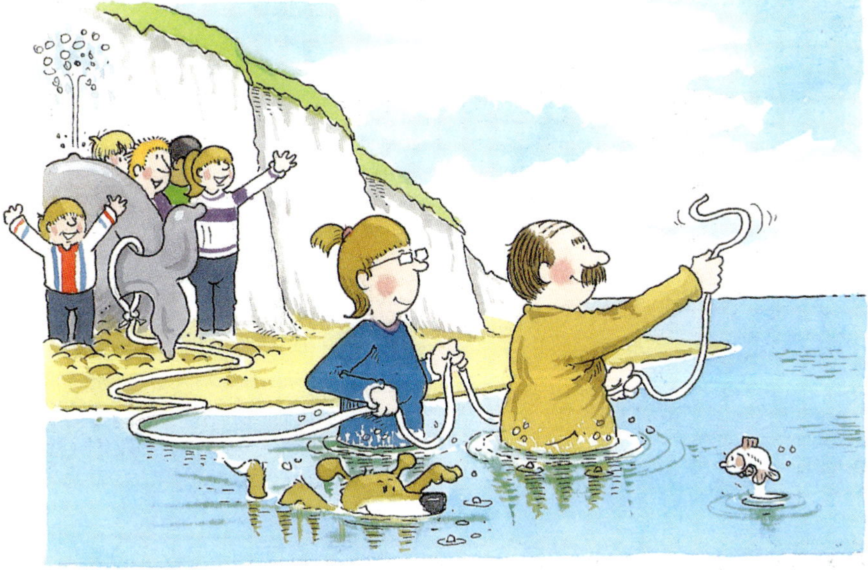

Miss Sim and Jack help Dad.

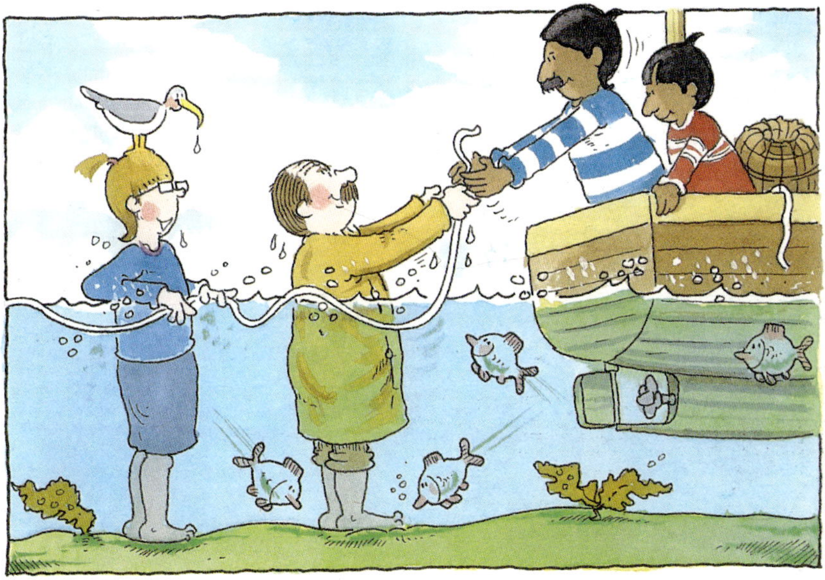

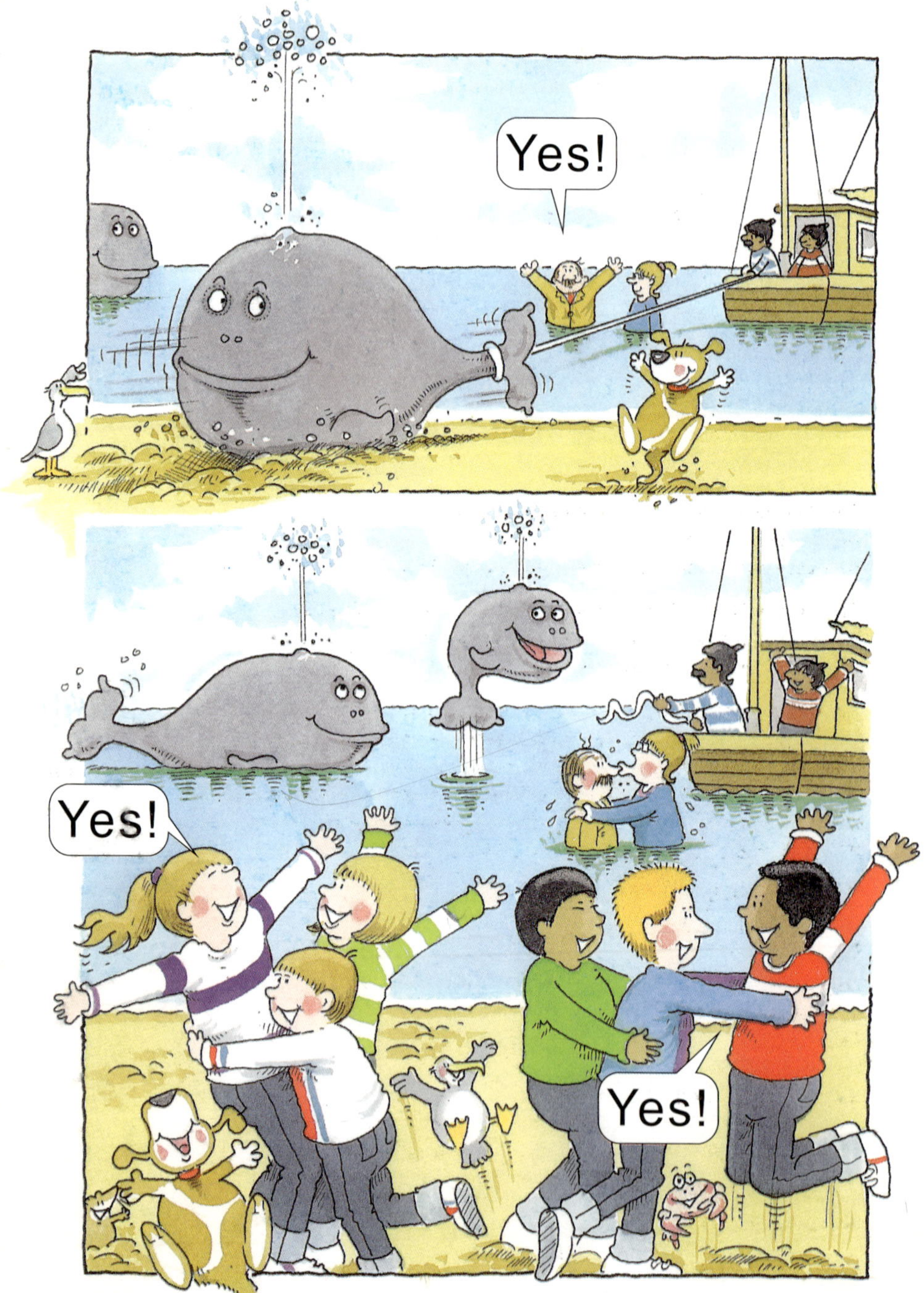
Yes!
Yes!
Yes!